MW01601344

The Five Traits of an Effective Intercessor

By
Bishop William H. Murphy, Jr.

This book is dedicated to my wife Donna and our wonderful children. Thank you for your untiring intercession for me.

Table of Contents

INTRODUCTION

As I read the exhortation of Paul to the church of Ephesus it became strikingly evident that beneath the writing was something I had never quite noticed before. Paul was speaking a word of intercession to those who could hear it. As I continued to read, it became clear that throughout scripture, Paul lived, taught and preached a life of prayer. What I saw was not Paul the great Apostle, Evangelist or Statesman but Paul as an Intercessor.

Paul was not just a preacher, but he was a type of Christ in the earth realm because of his work and ministry of Intercession. I looked at the letters of Paul and all throughout his writings you hear him saying; "I'm praying for you", "Pray without ceasing," "Praying always with all prayer and supplication". These are the exhortations of a man who understands the power of prayer.

By only looking at the life of Paul as a preacher we miss the true essence and power of his ministry. As an intercessor, we see the personal characteristics of courage, steadfastness, endurance, consecration, and self-sacrifice. Just as he possessed these unique attributes, every intercessor must have these same spiritual qualities. Paul stands as a great example of an intercessor.

As we look at the life and ministry of the Apostle Paul we can see the manifestation of his life of intercession through the accounts we read in the scriptures:

Acts 19:11 says,

And God wrought special miracles by the hands of Paul: This declares that God wrought special miracles by the hands of Paul, look at the next verse,

Acts 28:8 says,

And it came to pass, that the father of Publius lay sick of a fever and of a bloody flux: to whom Paul entered in, and prayed, and laid his hands on him, and healed him.

Open your bible for this next passage, in Acts 16:9-37; we can see a very clear picture of his operation in intercession.

In this passage we see the power, level and dimension that Paul operates on in Intercession. These verses prove the intercessory anointing of the Apostle Paul.

We see this manifesting through Paul's discernment of where the Spirit would have him to be or not to be in verse seven;

Acts 16:7-8 says,

After they were come to Mysia, they assayed to go into Bithynia: but the Spirit suffered them not. And they passing by Mysia came down to Troas.

We see it in the vision that he receives and also in his obedience to the vision in verse 9.

And a vision appeared to Paul in the night; There stood a man of

Macedonia, and prayed him, saying, Come over into Macedonia, and help us. And after he had seen the vision, immediately we endeavoured to go into Macedonia, assuredly gathering that the Lord had called us for to preach the gospel unto them. Therefore loosing from Troas, we came with a straight course to Samothracia, and the next day to Neapolis; And from thence to Philippi, which is the chief city of that part of Macedonia, and a colony: and we were in that city abiding certain days.

You can further see his discernment as it is exemplified in verse 13 in his ability to sense where prayer was made.

And on the sabbath we went out of the city by a river side, where prayer was wont to be made; and we sat down, and spake unto the women which resorted thither.

We see it in his ability to lead others to Christ in verse 14 –15 and we also see the spirit of intercession upon him as he deals with the damsel who was filled with the spirit of divination.

And a certain woman named Lydia, a seller of purple, of the city of Thyatira, which worshipped God, heard us: whose heart the Lord opened, that she attended unto the things which were spoken of Paul. And when she was baptized, and her household, she besought us, saying, If ye have judged me to be faithful to the Lord, come into my house, and abide there. And she constrained us.

And it came to pass, as we went to prayer, a certain damsel possessed with a spirit of divination met us, which brought her masters much gain by soothsaying: The same followed Paul and us, and cried, saying, These men are the servants of the most high

3

God, which shew unto us the way of salvation. And this did she many days. But Paul, being grieved, turned and said to the spirit, I command thee in the name of Jesus Christ to come out of her. And he came out the same hour.

Because of the anointing that was upon him for intercession the entire city became troubled, verses 19- 21,

And when her masters saw that the hope of their gains was gone, they caught Paul and Silas, and drew them into the marketplace unto the rulers, And brought them to the magistrates, saying, These men, being Jews, do exceedingly trouble our city, And teach customs, which are not lawful for us to receive, neither to observe, being Romans.

We see it in his ability to teach and also in his ability to suffer; they laid many stripes on him, cast him in prison in verses 21-24 and yet through all of these things even while in prison Paul still prays and sings hymns to God, thereby effecting not only the prisoners around him but shaking the very walls of the prison.

And the multitude rose up together against them: and the magistrates rent off their clothes, and commanded to beat them. And when they had laid many stripes upon them, they cast them into prison, charging the jailer to keep them safely: Who, having received such a charge, thrust them into the inner prison, and made their feet fast in the stocks. And at midnight Paul and Silas prayed, and sang praises unto God: and the prisoners heard them. And suddenly there was a great earthquake, so that the foundations of the prison were shaken: and immediately all the doors were opened, and every one's bands were loosed.

It is here that Paul intercedes for the keeper of the prison who would have killed himself had it not been for the prayer of Paul verse 27. Paul leads him to Christ by declaring unto them "Believe on Jesus Christ, and thou shalt be saved and thy house."

And the keeper of the prison awaking out of his sleep, and seeing the prison doors open, he drew out his sword, and would have killed himself, supposing that the prisoners had been fled. But Paul cried with a loud voice, saying, Do thyself no harm: for we are all here. Then he called for a light, and sprang in, and came trembling, and fell down before Paul and Silas, And brought them out, and said, Sirs, what must I do to be saved? And they said, Believe on the Lord Jesus Christ, and thou shalt be saved, and thy house. And they spake unto him the word of the Lord, and to all that were in his house. And he took them the same hour of the night, and washed their stripes; and was baptized, he and all his, straightway. And when he had brought them into his house, he set meat before them, and rejoiced, believing in God with all his house.

Because of the anointing that was on Paul we see his personal deliverance from prison but he also walks in the authority to establish and negotiate the criteria for his release.

And when it was day, the magistrates sent the sergeants, saying, Let those men go. And the keeper of the prison told this saying to Paul; The magistrates have sent to let you go: now therefore depart, and go in peace. But Paul said unto them, They have beaten us openly uncondemned, being Romans, and have cast us into prison; and now do they thrust us out privily? nay verily; but let them come themselves and fetch us out.

Paul was a man of prayer. We see it in every letter that he wrote throughout the scripture. He has given us our pattern for prayer in God's Word and from this we see the 5 traits of an effective intercessor:

1. He prays always.

2. He prays in the Spirit.

3. He is watchful.

4. He is unselfish.

5. He prays for leaders.

Over the next few chapters we will examine each of these traits and discover truths concerning each point. As we do, we will find that through our understanding increasing in these areas we will further dive into our intercessory purpose and destiny.

CHAPTER 1

AN EFFECTIVE INTERCESSOR ALWAYS PRAYS

Prayer is the supernatural provision of the Believer. It is through the prayers of the righteous that needs are met. Much of what is needed for the saints of God to move in their purpose and destiny is still waiting in glory, in the heavens, for some Believer to ask for it. Jesus says in Matthew 7:7

Ask, and it shall be given you; seek, and ye shall find; knock, and it shall be opened unto you:

This simple truth is the very basis for our communication with God. He stands waiting to open up the deep things to us if we would only ask. What makes this point so important is that through the words of *James 4:2-3* we see,

Ye lust, and have not: ye kill, and desire to have, and cannot obtain: ye fight and war; yet ye have not, because ye ask not. Ye ask, and receive not, because ye ask amiss, that ye may consume it upon your lusts.

It is evident that failure to understand what to ask for can hinder all of your attempts to move God through prayer. So what we must understand is that an effective intercessor always prays in the wisdom and in the will of God.

Luke 11:2 says,

And he said unto them, When ye pray, say, Our Father which art in heaven, Hallowed be thy name. Thy kingdom come. Thy will be done, as in heaven, so in earth.

Prayer brings forth the birthing of new and fresh revelation. It brings direction and insight and is the tool that gives us new strategies on the things that we must pray for. So, it is through prayer that we often find what we need to pray. This is why we must understand that our life is to be one in constant communication with God the Father through prayer. To do this we must commit to always praying. Jesus speaks this point plainly in Luke 18:1,

And he spake a parable unto them to this end, that men ought always to pray, and not to faint;

When I read this, immediately, I realized that there is a great danger in not always praying. I believe that what Jesus was saying was much deeper than what people really heard at the time and even more than what we hear today. We must realize that asking alone does not always reach the dimensions for our breakthroughs in the earth. There is sometimes more than one connection, or one breakthrough needed for total release. In other words, many times our deliverance is not merely in one prayer but many. Some situations that we find ourselves involved in must be prayed through from one point to another. It is the "praying through" to all of the points that will cause total breakthrough. One prayer alone may not cause the release that we need. It is from glory to glory; from faith to faith. As we pray revelation comes that will release us into the glory.

What I am saying is that you may have to get the revelation of the first thing, then the second; it is the revelation of the two together that will bring total deliverance. The enemy would love to trap you in a place where you simply pray through to the first revelation and quit, prior to the second, because you don't have the consistency to always pray.

To be sure that we don't miss it, we need to make sure that certain crucial elements are in place, which most importantly includes our committed preparation to specific times and locations for prayer.

If we fail to prepare, prayer will not just happen. There are times when we must stop and put things in place to walk in this anointing for prayer. We cannot move to this level of "always praying" haphazardly, it must be purposed through a committed lifestyle of prayer. The mindset of always praying is developed through your preparation. This is expressed through the words that David speaks to the people in 1 Chronicles 22:19 he says,

Now set your heart and your soul to seek the Lord your God; arise therefore, and build ye the sanctuary of the Lord God, to bring the ark of the covenant of the Lord, and the holy vessels of God, into the house that is to be built to the name of the Lord.

The focal point here is that the people "set" their hearts and their souls to seek the Lord. Think of the time, effort and energy they expended in preparing a place to commune with God. To set is "nathan" in the Hebrew, which is to appoint, to apply, to charge or to commit. What David was simply saying was that there must be a set place, an

9

appointed time or committed time that we seek the Lord. The beginning of this entire process was the committing of their hearts and souls to do it. There must be a tangible commitment before a Believer will position himself to pray always. Those who do not prepare their hearts will not carry out this command. There will always be something else that will take precedence over your duty to pray. I've come to know that the enemy will even use spiritual things to hinder you from praying. Know that he regularly uses the stuff of the church to cause the saints of God not to carry out this calling.

We must set our hearts and our souls for the work of the Lord. It will not happen merely because we are anointed to pray but we must have our hearts and souls directed towards prayer. If asked "what is your time to pray" and "where is your place to pray" what would your answer be? If you have no definite answer, then this may be a sign that you haven't adequately prepared to pray and could be missing it because time and place speak to the preparation of prayer. Throughout the scripture we see that God deals with specific times and places. We see this in phrases like "early" and "place".

Psalm 63:1 says,

A Psalm of David, when he was in the wilderness of Judah. O God, thou art my God; early will I seek thee: my soul thirsteth for thee, my flesh longeth for thee in a dry and thirsty land, where no water is;

Genesis 19:27 says,

And Abraham gat up early in the morning to the place where he stood before the Lord:

Both David and Abraham are known for their relationship with the Lord and their communion with him regularly. This carried out all throughout their lives. These men committed times and places to their seeking of the Lord through prayer. This is the pattern that we must follow if we are to develop our ability to pray always.

Again we see in Genesis 28:16-17 that Jacob is in a particular place and he awakes out of his sleep and says *"Surely the Lord is in this place; and I knew it not."*

He continues to say in verse 17, *"How dreadful is this place! this is none other but the house of God, and this is the gate of heaven."*

I believe that God is looking for particular places that he could place his name upon; places that are consecrated and set aside solely for communion with him. In chapter 35, Jacob establishes in this same place an altar unto the Lord.

Genesis 35:3 says,

And let us arise, and go up to Bethel; and I will make there an altar unto God, who answered me in the day of my distress, and was with me in the way which I went.

And it was there that God changes the name of Jacob to Israel. In this place he not only communes with God but he becomes the key vessel in God's promises to his fathers before him. I believe that this consistency of both place and time caused the release of his purpose and destiny.

As a Pastor, I remember that it was through designated places and times that we moved into the spirit of "always praying". Without even knowing that we were releasing this spirit upon the people, the Lord had us preparing times and places of prayer. This not only transformed the mind of those who were already praying but also those who had no prayer life at all. This opened me up to the power of preparation. It was the power of the preparation, the power of planning, which released us into this ministry of prayer. If we had never prepared for prayer, we would not be walking in this anointing. In every area of life, preparation makes for greater success, less stress, improved accuracy as well as empowerment. This also holds true for preparation in prayer.

Without preparation the church will never truly become the house of prayer. This is the time that we as people and as Believers must move beyond our traditions and move to a place of truly preparing to meet the Lord in prayer.

Besides preparing for prayer we must realize that it is our duty. This is another crucial element to making sure we always pray. Paul says in Ephesians 6:18,

Praying always with all prayer and supplication in the Spirit, and watching thereunto with all perseverance and supplication for all saints;

Paul expresses that the ministry of prayer is not an option

but a duty. Understanding that it is our duty to pray will help the intercessor to have the motivation to do what we are called to do and to do it consistently.

David when he sings his song of thanksgiving in 1 Chronicles 16:37 brings it to light for those who minister before the Lord. It says,

So he left there before the ark of the covenant of the Lord Asaph and his brethren, to minister before the ark continually, as every day's work required:

The scripture says, "as every day's work required". This speaks to Asaph and his brethren's duty; it was their responsibility, it was their job. At any point during the day you would expect that you would find them ministering before the Lord based on what the Word records. This was their daily work. We are to also take on this same attitude as we minister before the Lord through prayer. We must begin to look at prayer as an everyday work requirement.

We must begin to look at prayer as a duty and not as an extracurricular activity or something that we do when we are in trouble or in need. It is our responsibility to spend our lives and our time in prayer.

Duty is described in the Merriam Webster Dictionary as "obligatory tasks, conduct, service, or functions that arise from one's position (as in life or in a group)". This means that the task or responsibility comes not just as something to do but rather as a result of who we are. As the saints of God, He has assigned this responsibility to us, not only to pray always, but to pray understanding that this is the work of the Believer. In my book entitled *"How to Walk in a Victorious Prayer Life"* I describe the position of the Believer as one who takes on the responsibility of Christ in the earth realm as the intercessor. As he is in heaven, so are we in the earth.

1 John 4:17 says,

Herein is our love made perfect, that we may have boldness in the day of judgment: because as he is, so are we in this world.

With this understanding, our prayer lives should take on a new dimension. Hobbies are never usually followed up with the same consistency as our work. Many a person begins to tinker with the old 64 Buick in their garage, only finding that they never quite get back to it. But rarely, if ever, do you find someone who doesn't remember to get back to his or her job. They may take a long lunch, but I guarantee that they will eventually show back up to work.

This is how we are to look at our prayer lives. This is our duty, our work; but what a glorious work it is. Not one that is burdensome and tiring, but rather one that ushers us into the very presence of God. This responsibility allows us to gain wisdom from God himself for everything we need for today and tomorrow.

By taking on this level of commitment we will find that we will grow phenomenally into the intercessor God has called us to be. So then, we must receive this command from the Word as a part of who we are and what we have been called to do as Believers. Throughout the scriptures, not only are we commanded by Paul to pray as a duty but also, we see this command springing forth from others. Remember, we began with Jesus' words saying, "Men ought always to pray and not faint." The word Paul sends to the Thessalonian church is to "pray without ceasing." As Believers, this is who we are, and this is what we do. We are not who the tradition of the church says we are, such as, choir members, deacons and ushers only. Paul releases to us a different anointing than to simply be choir members, deacons and ushers; he releases to us the anointing to be people who pray. So then this is the work or the duty of the church of the living God.

What makes this so vital is that unless we see this as a duty we will have the calling and the burden and be so busy with other things that we neglect to pray. It's like I said about a hobby, it is far easier to let things crowd your plans when they are things that you view as optional. Duty compels a person to commitment. Therefore, you must see your call to pray as a call to duty. This is the driving force that pushes you to your purpose. Without seeing "praying always" as a duty we will miss our mark as true intercessors.

Paul in Ephesians 6:18 commands the Church, the Believer to pray always,

Praying always with all prayer and supplication in the Spirit, and watching thereunto with all perseverance and supplication for all saints;

The emphasis I want to focus on is "with all perseverance". To persevere is defined as "to persist in a state, enterprise, or undertaking in spite of counterinfluences, opposition, or discouragement." Paul, knowing that prayer was our duty, also stated that we must continue in prayer despite any and all opposition and hindrances to our responsibility. We must never cease or be turned back from this course of action.

This is the time that we as a people and as Believers must move beyond our traditions and move to a place of truly preparing to meet the Lord in prayer.

The greatest opposition to prayer for the intercessor right now is in the area of discipline. Our commitment to pray and to be good intercessors, not only manifests through praying consistently but also in the discipline of our body, mind and spirit. We must possess great discipline in order to become the intercessor that God is calling for in this season. Paul brings forth this revelation, he says 1 Cor. 9:24-27,

Know ye not that they which run in a race run all, but one receiveth the prize? So run, that ye may obtain. And every man that striveth for the mastery is temperate in all things. Now they do it to obtain a corruptible crown; but we an incorruptible. I therefore so run, not as uncertainly; so fight I, not as one that beateth the air: But I keep under my body, and bring it into subjection: lest that by any means, when I have preached to others, I myself should be a castaway.

The intercessor must be one of the most highly disciplined Believers within the body of Christ. Although every area of the body should be disciplined, because of the kind of warfare that is being waged, the intercessor must be more disciplined than them all. Other areas may be able to get away with being undisciplined, but this is an area where there must be complete discipline. This is an area where you can give no place to the Devil. This is the area where the enemy gives the church much trouble because we see the warfare as being all-spiritual. We are looking for all kinds of spooky stuff when the enemy attacks us in the area of our undisciplined body, mind and spirit. Paul declares and brings before us the revelation that we must be temperate in all things.

Always keep in mind that our bodies are the temples of the Holy Ghost and if the Devil can defeat your body, he can ultimately defeat the purpose of God in you.

1 Cor. 6:19-20 says,

What? know ye not that your body is the temple of the Holy Ghost which is in you, which ye have of God, and ye are not your own? For ye are bought with a price: therefore glorify God in your body, and in your spirit, which are God's.

The enemy knows that he cannot defeat the Spirit of God in you, so he works on your lack of discipline. The Devil wants to tear the temple down so that the Spirit does not have a vessel to use. Someone has to stand in the gap physically and you are the one.

It is difficult to get up when the Spirit calls when your body is suffering because of physical ailments and physical conditions. Doctors tell us that most of our conditions in our bodies are brought on by our lack of exercise, improper eating habits and lack of rest. You have to take natural care of yourself to insure that you *can* pray when you need to. Prayer is both spiritual as well as physical. God may have you on your knees, jumping, laying on the floor, walking and even running. So you have to be able to do all of this even as an effective athlete would. What a shame it is when the Spirit of God over takes us in prayer and we cannot respond because of the lack of discipline in our bodies.

Some might say that this is a hard word because it "doesn't take all of that" to talk to God, but I say to you, the Word tells us to lay aside every weight and hindrance that prevents us from the press. Needless to say, not only is lack of discipline in our bodies a weight but it will also rush us to our deaths. How does this honor God? How can we be an effective intercessor if we cut short 15 years of purposed prayers with our death? We must bring our bodies into subjection. We must begin to eat right, get plenty of sleep and exercise regularly. This is tied into our duty to pray. We have to be able to carry out this duty with the fullest vigor and determination required by the Lord.

I say to you that the enemy would love to use your undisciplined eating habits to cause your sicknesses that will impede your prayer life also. The Devil works through disorders that will slow you down and release spirits of heaviness that will cause you not to function, as you should. Things like diabetes and acid reflux will take away both your strength and your voice so that you cannot penetrate the heavens. These come through what is eaten; therefore, we must possess much discipline in the area of eating.

It is not by chance that throughout the scriptures we see prayer and lack of eating or no eating going hand in hand. It seems to me that when

you don't eat at all your body becomes the most pure, as well as the most holy. Your spiritual ears open and your vision and understanding are improved. Your discernment is clearer, your communion with God takes on new dimensions; even Christ, who was God's own son, spent time fasting and praying.

Matthew 17:21 says,

Howbeit this kind goeth not out but by prayer and fasting.

Mark 9:29 says,

And he said unto them, This kind can come forth by nothing, but by prayer and fasting.

These are two scriptures that give us a glimpse of the need of a prayer life that is filled with prayer and discipline.

The greater your discipline is; the greater your intercession will be. Don't let your lack of discipline with your body be the cause of missing your purpose and destiny.

The disciplined intercessor also must be careful what is in both mind and thought. Romans 12:1-2 says,

I beseech you therefore, brethren, by the mercies of God, that ye

present your bodies a living sacrifice, holy, acceptable unto God, which is your reasonable service. And be not conformed to this world: but be ye transformed by the renewing of your mind, that ye may prove what is that good, and acceptable, and perfect, will of God.

As intercessors, we must focus our minds on the prize; our concentration must be on the goal, which is the will of God being released in the earth. This must be the focus of the intercessor. We must forever bring forth strategies on how best to equip and position ourselves to win against the forces of Hell. By keeping our minds stayed on Him we will bring forth these strategies.

Our minds must become a disciplined place; a place where the Spirit of God can freely rule and reign. By not subduing our thoughts we will allow the enemy access to come in and get us off track with the very thoughts we think. The scripture tell us that we are to do this,

2 Cor. 10:5 says,

Casting down imaginations, and every high thing that exalteth itself against the knowledge of God, and bringing into captivity every thought to the obedience of Christ;

By exercising this type of discipline, we will reach greater levels of intercession. You have to take authority over your thought process and what you allow into your mind.

Proverbs 4:23 says,

Keep thy heart with all diligence; for out of it are the issues of life.

And again in James 4:7-8 it says,

Submit yourselves therefore to God. Resist the devil, and he will flee from you. Draw nigh to God, and he will draw nigh to you. Cleanse your hands, ye sinners; and purify your hearts, ye double minded.

We are accountable for the things that we entertain in our minds that will cause our hearts not to be pure. God is looking for a pure heart, a pure conscience. The psalmist knew the desire of God so he says in,

Psalm 51:6 says,

Behold, thou desirest truth in the inward parts: and in the hidden part thou shalt make me to know wisdom.

It is when our minds and hearts are pure that God fills our minds with His wisdom. This is why our minds must be clear so that we might be able to hear when He calls and to hear what He speaks. As an intercessor we must be able and in position for God to do what He desires to do.

To do this the mind of the intercessor must be filled with the Word of God. For the Word of God according to Hebrews 4:12 says,

...is quick, and powerful, and sharper than any two edged sword, piercing even to the dividing asunder of soul and spirit, and of the joints and marrow, and is a discerner of the thoughts and intents of the heart.

It is through knowing and practicing the Word of God that our minds are kept in perfect peace. It is through the use of scripture that we bring forth our greatest prayers; by upsetting the enemy and influencing God to move according to His will.

Therefore, we must read it, study it and allow it to subdue our minds. This will make us the type of intercessor that Christ is.

We must have our own mind issues settled. Those issues include low self-esteem, insecurities, fear, doubt, pride and so on. If you are weak in mind, then the enemy will be able to sift you as wheat. Peter, even though he was who he was, denied Christ because he had mind issues. He wasn't built up in the mind enough. He had too many thoughts of his own that were not the thoughts of God. Our thoughts are not our own but must remain in line with the will of God.

The runner and the athlete only has the race in his mind. How is he going to run it? How is he going to win it? How is he going to get the prize? To be effective, we must keep our minds focused on the race. This will cause us to be strong. Our race is to be consistent in prayer. By subduing our minds, we will win our race.

We must also remember that our bodies are the temples of the Holy Ghost we must always strive to keep his Spirit in place. We must stay in the Spirit; we must stay strong and motivated for the strength necessary for our work out day by day. This is necessary so that we may reach our goal. Prayer and warfare is a workout.

It is so easy to get tired, frustrated and overcome by the warfare. That is why the right spirit is so important. He that has the wrong spirit will not war an effective warfare. He is the power behind all that we do and say and without him we would be able to do nothing.

Covering our mind, which will ultimately cover the spirit, will allow intercession to remain a joy and a privilege. There are many who see intercession as a burden because they have not properly covered the thoughts they allow to linger in their mind because they don't maintain the right spirit for intercession, it becomes a burden. The Spirit teaches us how to pray and what to say when we don't know what we are to do. This is his job and we must maintain a right spirit so that we can commune with him. The bible tells us that the Holy Spirit will lead us into all truth and reveal to us the mind of Christ.

John 16:14-15 says,

He shall glorify me: for he shall receive of mine, and shall shew it unto you. All things that the Father hath are mine: therefore said I, that he shall take of mine, and shall shew it unto you.

How effective can we be when we try to pray out of our own mind and out of our own spirit? We need the help of the Holy Spirit to do this. Romans 8:26-27 says plainly,

Likewise the Spirit also helpeth our infirmities: for we know not what we should pray for as we ought: but the Spirit itself maketh intercession for us with groanings which cannot be uttered. And he that searcheth the hearts knoweth what is the mind of the Spirit, because he maketh intercession for the saints according to the will of God.

We must come to rely on the Holy Spirit to help us discipline ourselves in all areas. It is through depending on his work that we will be able to be the disciplined intercessor that will pray always.

For us our spirit should be one that is not haughty or proud, one that gives place for the Spirit to dwell with us and move through us. There can't be so much of us that there is no room for him. We must allow our spirit to be submitted to the Holy Spirit so that he can do what he has been sent to do. I will deal with this in more detail in the next chapter.

He must also be disciplined in the area of his regiment of prayer. I received this revelation one day, as I was going through the Holy Spirit said you cannot go in and out to battle with the enemy, either you are in or you are out. You cannot fight the enemy only when you get ready. Once you engage the enemy you must be ready always standing on guard and ready to go forth in battle. Once you engage you are open to the enemy. This is why you must enter the race to win. You must go in to win or else you will become a target to the enemy. The enemy's desire is to take you out. You must maintain discipline and cannot throw in the towel, by getting weak or complaining; you must remain strong.

1 Cor. 15:58 says,

Therefore, my beloved brethren, be ye steadfast, unmovable, always abounding in the work of the Lord, forasmuch as ye know that your labour is not in vain in the Lord.

Everything that we do as intercessors must point to the work of intercession that we are called to. We must always abound to the work of the Lord. We must be strong soldiers of the Lord.

An effective intercessor must also be open to new things. We cannot always do everything the same way. It is very easy in our commitment to pray always to become ritualistic and stuck in a prayer rut by only doing and expecting the same things.

This is ultimately locking you into a powerless prayer life and this weakened state will become your tradition. Our prayers must never become based on tradition but on the fresh revelation from the Spirit of God. Moses had to be open to hear from God out of the burning bush, which was not normal. Unless we are open to the abnormal or nontraditional, we just may position ourselves to miss God. We can see this in the life of Elijah as he went before the Lord.

1 Kings 19:11-12

And he said, Go forth, and stand upon the mount before the LORD. And, behold, the LORD passed by, and a great and strong wind rent the mountains, and brake in pieces the rocks before the LORD; but the LORD was not in the wind: and after the wind an earthquake; but the LORD was not in the earthquake: And after the earthquake a fire; but the LORD was not in the fire: and after the fire a still small voice.

Had Elijah been stuck on the wind or the earthquake or even the fire he would have never been open to hear the voice of God in a still small voice. He might have felt that something powerful happened in his time of waiting on the Lord but ultimately failed to see the results or learn the vital information that he did by hearing a new way.

1 Kings 19:18 says,

Yet I have left me seven thousand in Israel, all the knees which have not bowed unto Baal, and every mouth which hath not kissed him.

Elijah found that he wasn't the only one left serving the true and Living God and was encouraged to press on a little bit further. Imagine how bad his situation would have been if he had failed to hear God in the "new" way.

As intercessors, we must always be open to the move of God not to do it the same way it's been done. God will move for different situations in diverse kinds of ways and avenues. Had not Joseph been open to hear the voice of the Lord and leave the stable when he did, through the dream, the life of Christ may have been taken prematurely.

Matthew 2:12-13 says,

And being warned of God in a dream that they should not return to Herod, they departed into their own country another way. And when they were departed, behold, the angel of the Lord appeareth to Joseph in a dream, saying, Arise, and take the young child and his mother, and flee into Egypt, and be thou there until I bring thee word: for Herod will seek the young child to destroy him.

An open person changes plans in accordance with God's direction.

Similarly, after finding Jesus and worshiping him, the wise men being warned by the Holy Ghost that there were some things being released by the enemy, went back home another way. They were convinced by the Spirit not to go through Jerusalem as they had planned. This too spared the young life of Christ.

Whenever we deal with the Lord we must be ready to move and change our plans to match up with His.

There are times when we must be responsive and obedient to God's Word based on the fresh revelation that He gives through prayer. If you are locked into your tradition of prayer and hearing from God you will invalidate the true purpose of prayer in the first place.

There are times that I plan to pray for one thing and to go in one direction but can sense that God is doing something totally different than what I am trying to do. He may prompt me in a completely different direction than the one I had planned. These times are often the most powerful times I have in prayer because it has nothing to do with my preconceived ideas and desires but totally his will. Are you open enough and willing to be led a different way?

An open intercessor must be able to accept the unexpected. Divine guidance comes only to prepared hearts. What made

Joseph so important is that he remained receptive to God's guidance. Even though he was who he was, he did not think himself more highly than he should. We can never, as intercessors, close up and believe that we are the ones; it is always God. Remember that it is the Holy Spirit who leads us and directs us in prayer.

Romans 8:26 says,

Likewise the Spirit also helpeth our infirmities: for we know not what we should pray for as we ought: but the Spirit itself maketh intercession for us with groanings which cannot be uttered.

Conclusion

An effective intercessor will be sure that his lifestyle is one of always praying. He will guarantee this by constant preparation and dedication to set times and places of prayer. This is accomplished by understanding that this is our duty as Believers; prayer is not a choice for us, it is life to us. All of this is supported through a lifestyle of discipline in body, mind and spirit. Breaking off natural hindrances in our flesh will enable us to freely pray without the limitations of an unhealthy body. Controlling our thoughts will keep us clear to hear from God and disciplining our spirit will only propel us deeper into the will of God. Finally, we must remain open to the Lord at all times for all suggestion from the Spirit. This will allow us to be effective intercessors who always pray.

CHAPTER 2

AN EFFECTIVE INTERCESSOR MUST PRAY IN THE SPIRIT

One of the most awesome tools that we have been given is the access we have to the Holy Spirit. He lives in us and by his power we have access to the very heart and mind of God. We should at no time take for granted that fact. It is what has transformed us from the Old Testament saints to the New Testament "sons of God" filled with his Spirit and redeemed by his blood.

If we desire to be effective intercessors, we must realize the true power we have by accessing the Spirit in our prayer lives. I believe that when we talk about praying in the Spirit we have to look at more than simply praying in tongues or in our heavenly language. Praying in the Spirit is actually connecting to the mind of God and the will of God. The Bible tells us in I Corinthians 2:9-11,

But as it is written, Eye hath not seen, nor ear heard, neither have entered into the heart of man, the things which God hath prepared for them that love him. But God hath revealed them unto us by his Spirit: for the Spirit searcheth all things, yea, the deep things of God. For what man knoweth the things of a man, save the spirit of man which is in him? even so the things of God knoweth no man, but the Spirit of God.

This tells us a key fact, if we are to pray effectively,

according to the will of God, we need to know what His will is, and we know this by His Spirit.

The Bible tells us emphatically in James that often we find ourselves praying amiss because we don't know what to ask.

James 4:3 says, *Ye ask, and receive not, because ye ask amiss, that ye may consume it upon your lusts.*

When we pray without his direction or guidance, we are praying our own thoughts and ideas and there is no power behind the prayer. What intercessor wants to spend time praying with no reaction from Heaven? God is only responsible for that which is His will and desire. Let's look at what Jesus himself says in the famous Lord's Prayer, recorded in Matthew 6:9-13,

After this manner therefore pray ye: Our Father which art in heaven, Hallowed be thy name. Thy kingdom come, Thy will be done in earth, as it is in heaven. Give us this day our daily bread. And forgive us our debts, as we forgive our debtors. And lead us not into temptation, but deliver us from evil: For thine is the kingdom, and the power, and the glory, for ever. Amen.

In the simple words, *"Thy Kingdom come, Thy will be done on earth as it is in Heaven,"* we see the pattern for how we are to pray. It is not what we think that matters, but it is God's will that we need to line up with in our prayers. It is the Lord's desire that we pray in concert with what the Father has in mind, what His plans are and what His thoughts are for life and our situations. This is the way that we do this; by praying in His Spirit. We do not, of ourselves, have the ability to even comprehend the thoughts or mind of God. The Bible is emphatic, as it states in Isaiah 55:8-9

For my thoughts are not your thoughts, neither are your ways my ways, saith the LORD. For as the heavens are higher than the earth, so are my ways higher than your ways, and my thoughts than your thoughts.

It takes the power of the Lord and a special intervention from the Lord for us to even begin to comprehend His mind. The intercessor must come to understand this. Stop praying what you think and feel without the Spirit leading you in the direction that he wants to go in. Let your understanding be put aside for his greater will and purpose. To prevent being ineffective in prayer we must access the power of the Holy Spirit.

Most of us don't consider what happens when we pray out of the will of God or out of the Spirit. Often we will birth things contrary to the will of God. I have run into intercessors without the heart of God. You may find them praying that God kills someone when God wants them to live. Or likewise that God brings someone out of a situation that God wants them in for their eventual breakthrough.

Every situation is unique and requires a fresh sensitivity to the Spirit about the circumstance. You can't assume that what God said last year about this type of situation applies again. You have to do the Spirit test. Is your prayer out of love and long suffering or are you praying because you are tired of dealing with someone. Are you praying out of jealously, frustration and anger? We have to make sure we are praying out of the Spirit and his alone. We must search our hearts and ask ourselves, "Is this out of my flesh or of God? Whose will am I praying? Is it mine or his?"

Everything that He tells us will line up with His nature, His word and His character. Ask yourself "is this the nature of God?"

Many intercessors are now under the judgment of God because of their own character flaws hindering the will of God through their prayers. What they think or what they want. They often confuse the Spirit with being spooky. God is straightforward as is His Word and we must be careful as we walk this fine line in prayer.

The Bible tells us that every man must give an account to God. Matthew 12:35-37 says,

An Effective man out of the good treasure of the heart bringeth forth good things: and an evil man out of the evil treasure bringeth forth evil things. But I say unto you, That every idle word that men shall speak, they shall give account thereof in the day of judgment. For by thy words thou shalt be justified, and by thy words thou shalt be condemned.

This holds true for the intercessor. If we don't subdue our flesh and rely on His Spirit, we position ourselves to pray idle prayers. God will hold us responsible for birthing into the earth those things born out of our hurts, pains and disappointments. Therefore, it is imperative that we pray in the Spirit.

Like the prophet David prayed in Psalm 139:23-24, let this be our prayer also;

Search me, O God, and know my heart: try me, and know my thoughts: And see if there be any wicked way in me, and lead me in the way everlasting.

Even more than knowing the mind or will of God, the Spirit gives us access to the nature and character of God. This involves a deeper relationship with the Father to pray in His very nature and with the character of God. We understand His heart through the Spirit; the way that He feels about situations, about people and about issues. This is almost as important as knowing His will. By understanding His heart, we will more effectively pray even as He would; with the same passion and with the same drive.

Let's consider Jonah for a moment. He received a message from God for Nineveh. After his thwarted attempt to flee the will of God, he finally arrives and delivers the message. However, once the city repents, he finds himself angry with God for his choice of mercy. He didn't understand the heart of God concerning this people. Jonah 4:1-3 records,

But it displeased Jonah exceedingly, and he was very angry. And he prayed unto the LORD, and said, I pray thee, O LORD, was not this my saying, when I was yet in my country? Therefore I fled before unto Tarshish: for I knew that thou art a gracious God, and merciful, slow to anger, and of great kindness, and repentest thee of the evil. Therefore now, O LORD, take, I beseech thee, my life from me; for it is better for me to die than to live

Jonah prayed but he didn't understand the truth behind the way God felt for this people. He heard God concerning this city and interceded, in the sense that he stood on God's behalf declaring that destruction was coming. He stood in the gap; however, he failed to empathize with the one he represented. In fact, he was more concerned about the little gourd than the entire city with all of the people inside.

Jonah had a hard time breaking through to the will of God because of his own character flaw. Those who possess His Spirit must quickly forgive, have hope for the future and trust God to do what is the best in every situation, regardless of what we think about it. People with their own character issues will never tap into the will of God through prayer. They are locked into their flesh and therefore prevented for truly utilizing the Spirit for effective prayer. Our attitudes can even defile the thoughts of God and turn them into something never intended because of praying out of our flesh.

It is vital that we feel as he does if we are to be an effective intercessor. To simply pray words is to do a recital of prayer but to feel as He feels and pray as He would pray is to intercede; and this can only be done through the Holy Spirit.

When we look at the nature of God, we look at the Spirit that God moves and works out of; His motivating force, His character. Understanding this will help us become a more effective intercessor because we are to use His nature as a guide to ensure that our prayers line up with His Spirit. Let's look at what the Word tells us about the natures and characters of God.

It is clear that His nature is manifested through the fruits of the Spirit as we see them in Galatians 5:22-23, It says,

But the fruit of the Spirit is love, joy, peace, longsuffering, gentleness, goodness, faith, meekness, temperance: against such there is no law.

The fruit of the Spirit really shows us a clear picture of the God's character or His realm of operation. These are the motivating forces that drive Him in all that He does with His creation. So this is a very good place to begin to understand His Spirit.

The first thing listed is love. The bible tells us in John 3:16,

For God so loved the world, that he gave his only begotten Son, that whosoever believeth in him should not perish, but have everlasting life.

And again in I John 4:6-8 says,

We are of God: he that knoweth God heareth us; he that is not of God heareth not us. Hereby know we the spirit of truth, and the spirit of error. Beloved, let us love one another: for love is of God; and everyone that loveth is born of God, and knoweth God. He that loveth not knoweth not God; for God is love.

The very first song that we are taught in Sunday School is "Yes, Jesus Loves Me." This is the foundation of our faith and the reason that we stand justified by the blood of the Lamb, because of His love for us. How wrong it is for us then, as intercessors, to forget to let this be the motivating force behind all of our prayers. Even in prayers of judgment the cry of the Lord is always that they would receive His grace.

The intercessor stands perched in the gap for a God of love crying out to His people. Often, we carry this load in our hearts into prayer and it is through this love that we must find every prayer rooted. The Bible says that the spirit groans, the spirit longs; this is like a lover longing for the one he loves. This is to be your motivation in prayer, that they would see Him, that they would love Him, that they would avoid the trappings of the enemy. All birthed out of the Spirit that is driven by love.

The next fruit is that of Joy. Romans 14:17 says, *For the kingdom of God is not meat and drink; but righteousness, and peace, and joy in the Holy Ghost.*

Acts 13:52 says,

And the disciples were filled with joy, and with the Holy Ghost.

There is supposed to be a correlation of Joy and the Holy Spirit. It is part of His nature and should become part of ours. Often we think that to be deep and spiritual we must be dry and stuffy and sedate and we fail to allow God's own joy to flow through us. The Bible tells us in Nehemiah 8:10, *for the joy of the LORD is your strength.*

And as we discussed in chapter 1 you need natural and spiritual strength to sustain through prayer. So be sure to allow the Holy Spirit to birth His joy in you. Often you will find Believers bursting out in holy laughter from the overwhelming fullness of joy that they feel. Don't be alarmed when you find this happening in your prayer times. Pure joy will overflow and change the way you respond in prayer but it is just as important as when you are in a time of travail.

Longsuffering is something that we see throughout scripture and often times forget because we focus on the judgment of God. Over and over we see that when their sin had reached its full measure God would come in and do something. He always gave them time to repent. He sent prophets to warn. He sent His Word and, of course, He sent His Son. From Old to New Testament we see a God patiently pleading, watching, waiting and loving. The very definition of the word longsuffering means, patient and enduring in the face of suffering or difficulty.

This is God's nature. Don't mistakenly think that because you see on one page the children of Israel cutting up and on the next judgment coming that it all occurred in the time it took you to turn the page. Often hundreds of years have passed by; all the while our loving God has endured difficulty in seeing His covenant people living beneath their means.

His full intent, when He brought the children of Israel from Egypt, was for them to go into the Promised Land. They chose to believe a lie and missed out. God continued to deal with them and their unbelief because of His longsuffering and some powerful intercessory prayers made by Moses.

Gentleness and goodness go hand in hand. They speak to His ways of dealing with his people. Isaiah 40:11 says *He shall feed his flock like a shepherd: he shall gather the lambs with his arm, and carry them in his bosom, and shall gently lead those that are with young.*

He even calls himself the Good Shepherd in John 10:11 *I am the good shepherd: the good shepherd giveth his life for the sheep.*

He is a good God who, though he doesn't tolerate sin, is filled with compassion and goodness towards His creation. His actions are good and His thoughts are good towards us. This will also be one of the many roots of our prayer life in the spirit, goodness and gentleness.

The fact that faith is a fruit of the Spirit means that the ability for belief is something that emanates from God Himself. The scripture is very clear about the importance of faith. In Hebrews 1:1 we find its definition which says,

Now faith is the substance of things hoped for, the evidence of things not seen.

Faith is what brings our prayers to life and the source for that faith comes from the Spirit. The intercessor will find that as we stand in prayer, we must have the faith to believe those things that the Spirit has given us to pray. We also must have faith to access the Spirit; this makes this a key element in the life of the praying Believer.

In verse 6 of the same chapter it says

But without faith it is impossible to please him: for he that cometh to God must believe that he is, and that he is a rewarder of them that diligently seek him.

Our need for accessing the faith of God goes beyond even our ability to pray effectively. It is the source of our being pleasing to God. He honors us and rewards us based on our faith and our faith is birthed for yielding to the Holy Spirit that is at work in us.

Showing mildness or quietness of nature is the definition. This speaks more to His character. His nature isn't boisterous and brash. He is who He is, but He manifest His greatness through meekness. He doesn't have to assert Himself. Matthew 11:28-30 says,

Come unto me, all ye that labour and are heavy laden, and I will give you rest. Take my yoke upon you, and learn of me; for I am meek and lowly in heart: and ye shall find rest unto your souls. For my yoke is easy, and my burden is light.

How often do we see those in prayer given to stealing the show or praying to be seen of men? We all know how Jesus felt about those praying to be seen, Matthew 18:10-18

Two men went up into the temple to pray; the one a

Pharisee, and the other a publican. The Pharisee stood and prayed thus with himself, God, I thank thee, that I am not as other men are, extortioners, unjust, adulterers, or even as this publican. I fast

twice in the week, I give tithes of all that I possess. And the publican, standing afar off, would not lift up so much as his eyes unto heaven, but smote upon his breast, saying, God be merciful to me a sinner. I tell you, this man went down to his house justified rather than the other: for every one that exalteth himself shall be abased; and he that humbleth himself shall be exalted.

To be an effective intercessor we are to pray in the spirit of meekness.

Temperance is the final fruit of the Spirit and it speaks to control. We are not to be people without order or control. His Spirit is always tempered and never out of His established order. By allowing the fruit of the Spirit to be your guide as you intercede, you will find the help you need to prevent many pitfalls of prayer.

These are the natures that as intercessors we are to pray in and out of. When we pray in these fruits, we know that as we pray the Spirit is at work in us. One of the failures of many intercessors is that they do not pray out of the right Spirit. Everything that the Father and Son have done in the earth has been out of these fruits.

Praying in the Spirit also releases revelation. You may ask the question what is *revelation*? The word revelation comes from the Greek word, "apokalupsis", meaning to unveil, to uncover or to reveal truth. Light must be translated into the human thought in order for us to comprehend, understand and or to remember. Revelation must be expressed in thought if we are to gain understanding. Only the spirit man can understand or receive revelation. John 16:13 says,

Howbeit when he, the Spirit of truth, is come, he will guide you into all truth: for he shall not speak of himself; but whatsoever he shall hear, that shall he speak: and he will shew you things to come.

Praying in the Spirit, releases the living Word of God. It quickens us and gives us faith to believe God. It also creates in us a spiritual appetite to hear from God. The Spirit helps you apply the Word of God into your everyday life and with it creates great expectancy because it feeds the inner man.

So, praying in the Spirit, helps restore man to God. Man cannot live a holy life, independent from God; there must be a connection in the Spirit. If we never pray in the realm of the Spirit, we are limited to communication only in our territorial tongue.

God created man to have fellowship with Him and without His direction we would be lost. Proverbs 20:24 says,

Man's goings are of the LORD; how can a man then understand his own way?

Praying in the Spirit, leads us into a new dimension of the Spirit in prayer, this is a major key to enter into intercessory prayer, and this opens our channels of communication. Isaiah 1:18 calls out,

Come now, and let us reason together, saith the LORD: though your sins be as scarlet, they shall be as white as snow; though they be red like crimson, they shall be as wool.

Through the death of His Son He has made a way for us to

commune with Him on a daily basis.

The secret of praying effectively in the Spirit is having a sincere desire and love for God and His People. Jesus said, *"Blessed are they who do hunger and thirst for righteousness, they shall be filled."* We must choose to be dependent upon God.

Conclusion

As an effective intercessor, we must understand it is through the Spirit we are made effective teachers, and effective teachers, make effective witnesses for Christ. Our new nature arises within the very person that did not know God. He fills our lives with His resurrection power to make us what we are destined to be, the Spirit fulfills us. He unfolds His plans and purpose to us in the realm of the Spirit, the call to intercession transforms our lives in the Spirit realm.

By accessing the Spirit we become more effective because we receive the knowledge of the will of God and revelation concerning the situations we intercede for. We also tap into His very nature and heart through the Spirit. To be an effective intercessor we must always pray in the Spirit.

CHAPTER 3

AN EFFECTIVE INTERCESSOR MUST BE WATCHFUL IN THE SPIRIT

After establishing the foundation for praying always and praying in the Spirit, these next few chapters will go much quicker. The need for an intercessor to constantly be at their work and to do it with the Spirit may seem obvious; but the next three points are crucial as well. To be an effective intercessor you must be watchful in the Spirit.

You may ask yourself, what kinds of things do we as intercessors need to watch for? Well let's first ask the question, what does it mean to be watchful? This word implies to stay awake, not to sleep, and to be carefully observant or alert.

Christ is our great example of all that a true intercessor is and his very nature was that of watchfulness. We hear him saying in Matthew 26:41,

Watch and pray, that ye enter not into temptation: the spirit indeed is willing, but the flesh is weak.

This indicates to us that as we pray we must also be mindful that the enemy is still planning to war against us, that the warfare is not over because we have decided to enter into this time of intercession. One of the most spiritual times for a Believer is during his time of intercession; but of course what better time for the enemy to sneak in an attack upon the Believer as well. If you are ever open to possible attack it is during your time of intercession. In this, your most spiritual time, you need to be more watchful than at any other.

1 Peter 5:7-8 says,

Casting all your care upon him; for he careth for you. Be sober, be vigilant; because your adversary the devil, as a roaring lion, walketh about, seeking whom he may devour:

This is his constant posture, one of a lion but read it carefully for he is only "like a lion," if he finds you unaware and not watchful he will definitely pounce on you.

As intercessors we must always be tapped into to the dimension of God through prayer. Here again we see the Apostle Paul's exhorting us to be watchful in prayer.

1 Corinthians 11:27 says he possessed the spirit of watchfulness and it was a part of his personal struggles, it says,

In weariness and painfulness, in watchings often, in hunger and thirst, in fastings often, in cold and nakedness.

Looking at Paul's life we understand why he was in this state of watching but though we are not under the penalty or possible death for operating in our calling we must be ever vigilant to watch in prayer. Paul declares to the saints to pray in the spirit but to also watch. I found that this is no different than what Jesus asked his disciples to do.

Perhaps the reason this is so vital is that it is dangerous for the intercessor to leave this most spiritual place.

Matthew 24:48-51 says,

But and if that evil servant shall say in his heart, My Lord delayeth his coming; And shall begin to smite his fellow servants, and to eat and drink with the drunken; The Lord of that servant shall come in a day when he looketh not for him, and in an hour that he is not aware of, And shall cut him asunder, and appoint him his portion with the hypocrites: there shall be weeping and gnashing of teeth.

There are two clear reasons why we must be watchful in prayer. One is because of the attack of the enemy and the other is to be ready for the move of God, both now and for his coming or return.

Luke 12:41-44 shows us the need for watchfulness so that we don't miss the move of God. The very thing that you could have been waiting for in prayer can be missed for your

lack of watchfulness. When God is ready to release it you must be in position to receive it. Jesus makes it clear when he ministers to Peter in this passage. It says,

then Peter said unto him, Lord, speakest thou this parable unto us, or even to all? And the Lord said, Who then is that faithful and wise steward, whom his Lord shall make ruler over his household, to give them their portion of meat in due season? Blessed is that servant, whom his Lord when he cometh shall find so doing. Of a truth I say unto you, that he will make him ruler over all that he hath.

I believe that as intercessors our mission and purpose is to watch. God speaks this clearly in Ezekiel.

Ezekiel 3:17 says,

Son of man, I have made thee a watchman unto the house of Israel: therefore hear the word at my mouth, and give them warning from me.

God told him that it was his job and purpose to watch over the House of Israel and to stand as an intercessor as he did so. This call was not just to him but to us all.

As intercessors we must be watchful so that we might catch what God is doing for a particular people at a particular time. We cannot afford to miss the move of God in behalf of those whom we serve.

Mark 13:34 records,

For the Son of man is as a man taking a far journey, who left his house, and gave authority to his servants, and to every man his work, and commanded the porter to watch.

To watch will help you as an intercessor to identify change or the time for change. Not just in the church but in the nation and in your personal lives. To watch must be a lifestyle as well as your prayer life. If we as intercessors are not watching Satan will take advantage of us

1 Corinthians 2:11 says,

Lest Satan should get an advantage of us: for we are not ignorant of his devices.

To watch and pray means that we are with knowledge or understanding of what our enemy, Satan, is doing. God has warned us to not be ignorant of what he will use against us, therefore, we must watch. And it is through prayer that God is able to reveal Satan's schemes to us. If we fail to watch Satan will take what rightfully belongs to us.

Let's look at the following scriptures,

Ephesians 6:18 says,

Praying always with all prayer and supplication in the Spirit, and watching thereunto with all perseverance and supplication for all saints;

1 Peter 5:8 says,

Be sober, be vigilant; because your adversary the devil, as a roaring lion, walketh about, seeking whom he may devour:

Again and again we are encouraged to watch. Here is an example of what happens when we fail to watch,

Isaiah 56:10 says,

His watchmen are blind: they are all ignorant, they are all dumb dogs, they cannot bark; sleeping, lying down, loving to slumber.

This passage warns of the blind watchman. An intercessor that finds themselves in this position will be of no value in prayer.

The key here is that it ties into the sensitivity of the Spirit but it also speaks to our posture as intercessors. We are to be ever alert and listening and looking for signs for prayer. The signs may come as warnings or promptings, they may come through what we see around us in the news but they are always there. God is forever trying to make sure that we are not taken unaware of anything. If you really think about it, God may have been trying to tell you many things that would have helped you in the past, but by failing to be watchful you missed them only to realize it later.

This is the very thing he doesn't want to happen. He doesn't want us to see after the attack or after the need for prayer has passed. He wishes that we have knowledge prior to things so that we can change them.

Hosea 4:6 says,

My people are destroyed for lack of knowledge: because thou hast rejected knowledge, I will also reject thee, that thou shalt be no priest to me: seeing thou hast forgotten the law of thy God, I will also forget thy children.

This tells us we can be destroyed for our lack of knowledge. And knowledge in prayer can only come from our watchfulness.

A good example of a failure to watch can be found in the first book of the Bible. We see that Adam failed to watch Eve and the whole of creation came under a curse for his failure. We must never take anything for granted during times of prayer and during our day to day activities; on the job, in the car and at church. We must remain watchful and poised to be aware for what may come our way.

Conclusion

It is necessary that if we are to be effective in our prayer lives, we must watch and pray. It is through this watching that we will be made aware of the attack and tactics of the enemy against ourselves and the people of God. It is also where we need to be found as we sense the times and seasons going on around us. God is looking for those who will agree to be the watchman on the wall over His bride, His people and His creation. Those committed to live and pray on alert will be those who will take their prayer lives to another dimension.

CHAPTER 4

AN EFFECTIVE INTERCESSOR MUST PRAY UNSELFISHLY

Because of the nature of the intercessor many mistakenly take on an air of superiority because of hearing from God, and being in position to affect change in the earth. If they have followed the information in the previous chapter's they would realize that to pray in the flesh will nullify the work that they are attempting in the first place. We cannot wear intercession as a coat of glory or righteousness. Some think that we can use this as a way to qualify ourselves better than everyone else. But it is vital that we keep things in perspective.

Romans 12:3 says,

For I say, through the grace given unto me, to every man that is among you, not to think of himself more highly than he ought to think; but to think soberly, according as God hath dealt to every man the measure of faith.

Those that will operate in the Spirit of intercession must always walk and move in a humble spirit.

I believe that so many disqualify themselves because they approach the throne and the presence of God with the wrong attitude. Again let's look at the story of the publican. In Luke 18:10-11 it says,

Two men went up into the temple to pray; the one a Pharisee, and the other a publican. The Pharisee stood and prayed thus with himself, God, I thank thee, that I am not as other men are, extortioners, unjust, adulterers, or even as this publican.

This man thought more of himself than he should have. He felt that even during a time of approaching God that he was somehow better than this other man.

Luke 18:13 shows us the picture of the humble it says,

and the publican, standing afar off, would not lift up so much as his eyes unto heaven, but smote upon his breast, saying, God be merciful to me a sinner.

This is the attitude that we are to have. Notice that Christ himself commends this man for his contrite Spirit. Prayer cannot be about our person, character or our flesh. It is when we take ourselves out of the picture and pray unselfishly that we become more effective.

Notice the attitude of Christ as it relates to Philippians 2:7 it says,

but made himself of no reputation, and took upon him the form of a servant, and was made in the likeness of men:

Christ was one who made no reputation for himself, he never took on the spirit of trying to be somebody or trying to make like he was better than the rest. The Bible tells us in Colossians 1:15-19 that,

Who is the image of the invisible God, the firstborn of every

creature: For by him were all things created, that are in heaven, and that are in earth, visible and invisible, whether they be thrones, or dominions, or principalities, or powers: all things were created by him, and for him: And he is before all things, and by him all things consist. And he is the head of the body, the church: who is the beginning, the firstborn from the dead; that in all things he might have the preeminence. For it pleased the Father that in him should all fulness dwell;

If Christ humbled himself, who are we to even begin to think more highly than we ought. Our savior teaches this important lesson and it is a truth that every intercessor must remember to walk in.

Paul exemplifies this same nature and character throughout his writings. I noticed that it was always about others and never about him. His ministry was always focused on other people's situations and relationships with the Father. When someone finds that everything is about them, they become selfish.

This subject is important because if you possess the spirit of selfishness you will never look at or stand in the gap for others. Those who have this selfish spirit will always be focused on themselves. Selfishness, in and of itself, nullified the very purpose of the intercessor, one who stands in the gap for others.

We must remember that no flesh will at any time glory in the presence of the Lord. Christ said, "I did not come to be ministered to, but I came to minister to others." We must have this same Christ like Spirit. Intercession has to always be concentrated on others.

Effective intercession must always be done in the right Spirit. It must always be done according to the will of the Father in heaven. Jesus' cry was, as he would stand in the gap for all mankind, "not mine will but thy will be done". This is the cry of every true intercessor.

The intercessor must always be careful not to pray selfishly or according to their will, desire or selfish motives. An effective intercessor always prays according to the will of God. Not simply because a thing looks right or wrong, for there is a way that seemeth right.

Proverbs 14:12 says,

There is a way, which seemeth right unto a man, but the end thereof are the ways of death.

We must always be open to the reality that what seems right to us may not be right with God and what may seem wrong to us may be the plan of God in the earth. I have come to know that when we pray with a selfish Spirit that the enemy will use this door as a way to cause the Believer to pray out of the will of God. Selfishness will lead you out of the will of God.

This selfish praying, releases you into a place where you start to pray against the work and plan of God in the earth and begin to release your own thoughts and will in the earth. There are times when I am unsure about what God wants to do in the earth so my prayer is simply *'Thy will be done on earth as it is in heaven. God I'm just lining up with you, open doors that should be open, and close every door that shouldn't be open. When I get the revelation of what you are doing then I will pray more specially so as not to be coming against God.'*

An effective intercessor never prays out of what he or she thinks, seeks or desires, it is all about God's will in the earth. We must always remember that we are a vehicle used by God in the earth to release His will in the heavens into the earth. Once we lose this purpose we have lost our place and role as one who stands in the gap as an intercessor. The intercessor is not "his own tool" but a tool in the hands of God. This is why communication with God is so important. John 15 shows us just how important our connection is, for without him I am nothing.

John 15: 16 says,

Ye have not chosen me, but I have chosen you, and ordained you, that ye should go and bring forth fruit, and that your fruit should remain: that whatsoever ye shall ask of the Father in my name, he may give it you.

John 15 gives us three truths that we need to understand as we stand in the gap as intercessors. I am who I am because of him. I am in the know because of my connection to him and I lose who I am when I become myself or operate in the spirit of selfishness.

Knowing that He has chosen us and that we did not choose ourselves keeps us out of the realm of selfishness. It is here that we can see that we have no leverage on anyone. We understand that it is by God's mercy and grace that we are positioned in the gap where we are. That it is not that our life has been any better than others, but that God has seen fit to make us what we could have never been on our own.

Philippians 2:13 says,

For it is God which worketh in you both to will and to do of his good pleasure.

I have come to know that it is God who has been keeping me and not my own power. If it were not for the hand of God, I would have fallen a long time ago, but praises be to God, our keeper. I believe that every Believer, without the aid of the Holy Spirit, is only one step away from a great fall, therefore, my prayer is Lord keep me, Lord cover me, Lord don't allow the enemy to have his way with me. We must realize that it is God's power and not ours.

Jude 1:24 says,

Now unto him that is able to keep you from falling, and to present you faultless before the presence of his glory with exceeding joy,

Once you lose sight of this you become open and vulnerable to failure. You are who you are today only because of Him. This is why an effective intercessor never gets caught in selfishness and never points the finger. This is why he is always looking to God for all answers and in all things praying in His will. The Spirit placed this in my spirit as I was meditating; selfishness is lowliness.

Once we begin to operate in the Spirit of selfishness we leave our place in the gap and we come down, ultimately losing who we are in Christ. We are not the same person operating in Christ as we are operating out of Christ; he says *without me ye can do nothing*. I am what I am because of Christ, when I operate under my own power I fail to operate in Him and become subject to miss the will of God. I am a part of Him and operate in His anointing, so He says *I am the vine and ye are the branches.*

John 15:4-5 says,

Abide in me, and I in you. As the branch cannot bear fruit of itself, except it abide in the vine; no more can ye, except ye abide in me. I am the vine, ye are the branches: He that abideth in me, and I in him, the same bringeth forth much fruit: for without me ye can do nothing.

As I stand in the gap I stand in Him and there is no room for selfishness or no room, should I say, for me.

Selfishness takes us out of the gap and causes us to lose our connections. When we lose our connection this also causes us to lose our communication. This causes us to lose our insight and revelation. We only know what we know because we are in place in the gap between the earth and the heavens. We have this privilege because of our connection to him.

It is important to know that when we lose the connection because of operating in the wrong Spirit we will also lose our insight and revelation. Jesus makes mention of this connection in John 17, He says in verse 6 through 8,

I have manifested thy name unto the men which thou gavest me out of the world: thine they were, and thou gavest them me; and they have kept thy word. Now they have known that all things whatsoever thou hast given me are of thee. For I have given unto them the words which thou gavest me; and they have received them, and have known surely that I came out from thee, and they have believed that thou didst send me.

He shows us the connection again in John 17:22-23,

And the glory which thou gavest me I have given them; that they may be one, even as we are one: I in them, and thou in me, that they may be made perfect in one; and that the world may know that thou hast sent me, and hast loved them, as thou hast loved me.

Those who operate in Him will receive the secret things of God through His son Jesus Christ. The revelation comes as a result of our connection with the Christ. The Spirit of Christ was a humble Spirit and it is when no revelation is being released that we must check for the Spirit of selfishness.

As an effective intercessor we must understand that we know what we know not because of us but because of our relationship with Him. This truth and attitude will keep us in a humble position, because we cannot afford to lose relationship.

Romans 8:26 says,

Likewise the Spirit also helpeth our infirmities: for we know not what we should pray for as we ought: but the Spirit itself maketh intercession for us with groanings which cannot be uttered.

Again, in John 16:13 says,

Howbeit when he, the Spirit of truth, is come, he will guide you into all truth: for he shall not speak of himself; but whatsoever he shall hear, that shall he speak: and he will shew you things to come.

I lose who I am in Christ when I began to operate in the Spirit of selfishness. Selfishness cancels out the Christ in you and causes you to be controlled by your own thoughts, desires, motives, ambitions and agendas. These have no place in the kingdom and cause us to operate outside of the will of God. When Jesus said pray to the Father, it was as if he were saying in so many words, stay focused on God and what's in the heavens. When the focus turns to self, our prayer becomes low and beneath the will of God. It is the spirit of selfishness that breaks the connection between the intercessor and Christ.

This causes the church, the body of Christ and the Believer to move into places, to do things, to receive things that God intended to be inactive in the earth. This includes thoughts, attitudes and spirits. I believe that this is what causes us to lose our close fellowship with the Father and to seek our own directions. Because of this many intercessors become lying prophets having no real word from the Lord.

God cannot trust those who walk and operate in the Spirit of selfishness. And only those who truly stand in the gap can be trusted, in deed.

I have seen with my own eyes those who have broken the connection, many of which have become spiritual vagabonds; once great and mighty men and women of God. The Spirit of selfishness will cause the intercessor to become a drifter in the kingdom never being able to get in the right place because of this Spirit. This Spirit reduces us to the same state as a sinner and God waits for acceptance of the Spirit of repentance so that He might release a Spirit of restoration. This only happens when one moves out of self and looks to the Lord who is the author and finisher of our faith.

Selfishness will always open us up to a self-righteous Spirit, but we must remember that our righteousness is in Him. When we lose this relationship we also lose the Spirit of righteousness and in the meantime lose His presence.

Charles Dawes tells the story of how an appointment was lost by selfishness.

President McKinley was considering the appointment of a minister to a foreign country. There were two candidates, their qualifications almost equal. Which one did he appoint? The President related a story of an incident that had decided his choice:

Years before, when he was a Representative, he boarded a streetcar one night and took the last vacant seat. Shortly afterward, an old washerwoman entered carrying a heavy basket. She walked the length of the car and stood in the aisle, no one offering her a seat.

One of the men, whom the President was to consider later, was sitting in a seat opposite where she was standing. He shifted the paper so as not to see her. Mr. McKinley walked down the aisle, picked up her basket of washing, and gave her his seat. The candidate never knew that this little act of selfishness had deprived him of perhaps the crowning honor of a lifetime.

How much more does selfishness block the blessing of the Lord from our lives? Remember that He is ever watching the motives and intents of our hearts.

Conclusion

We must remember that we are only who we are to carry out and to release the will of God into the earth. Therefore, we must keep our Spirit checked to make sure our hearts and minds are pure and clean from a Spirit of selfishness. When this door is opened the enemy will have intercessors praying for things that are not according to the will of God. To be most effective we must rid ourselves of our flesh and humbly say, *"not my will but thy will be done."*

CHAPTER 5

AN EFFECTIVE INTERCESSOR MUST PRAY FOR LEADERS

One area that I feel we must address to become an effective intercessor is that of praying for those in authority. It is found throughout scripture but often is overlooked. This is something that we must master if we are to become good intercessors.

Paul exhorts us to pray for those who have the rule over us, in 1 Timothy 2:1-3 he says,

I exhort therefore, that, first of all, supplications, prayers, intercessions, and giving of thanks, be made for all men; For kings, and for all that are in authority; that we may lead a quiet and peaceable life in all godliness and honesty. For this is good and acceptable in the sight of God our Saviour;

Paul leads us here in this verse to pray for leaders in particular. The question you may have is why pray for leaders, why focus on leaders and not necessary upon the whole church. This does not to say that there isn't a time to pray for the church or the Body of Christ for there is, but there is a special anointing attached to our leaders. As we look though the scriptures it becomes evident that we must pray for our leaders.

Nations, countries, churches, and ministries rise and fall at the hands of those who lead. The quality of the leader will determine the quality of the nation. An effective intercessor hears the cry of leadership and understands the need for praying for those who rule or those who are in authority.

There are three areas for the effective intercessor to understand when considering the need of prayer for leadership. He must first understand the need, secondly, he must understand the call, and thirdly, he must understand the purpose.

Let's take a look at understanding the need.

Intercessors as we established are also watchmen, and needed in the body of Christ as those who would watch over the man and woman of God. For several years before this writing I was having trouble with my mouth. One of our Elders, who serves as our director of protocol, noticed a pattern. Her revelation of what was going on with my mouth taught me a lot, mainly that there is a need for someone to pay attention to the man or woman of God both physically and spiritually. Her revelation was very simple but yet very true and very powerful. It was that every year around the same time usually towards the end of the year mainly October or November that the same attack would take place. I believe that these attacks could be warded off with a plan of prayer. Every year, around the same time, intercessors should be on the watch praying against the attack that seemingly came again and again.

This brings before us the truth that there are those who need to stand in the gap as watchmen, watching and praying for the man or woman of God. There will be things that you may see or discern that need to be defended for the man or woman of God, which they don't see.

Jesus saw the enemy's attack coming upon Peter even before Peter knew that the enemy could attack him in that area. Even though Peter was saying, thinking and believing that "I could never deny the Christ," Jesus as an intercessor saw what was going to happen even before Peter was moved by the spirit of denial.

Luke 22:31-32 says,

And the Lord said, Simon, Simon, behold, Satan hath desired to have you, that he may sift you as wheat: But I have prayed for thee, that thy faith fail not: and when thou art converted, strengthen thy brethren.

Jesus stood in the gap; therefore, Peter was able to be a blessing to others when he was converted. God needs intercessors positioned to see what the man and woman of God is not positioned to see. Peter was able to come through because he was covered in prayer.

In intercession there is what is called spiritual mapping. This is when territories are surveyed to see what Spirit or Spirits operate in a particular area. This can also be done in the area of leadership; I refer to it as spiritual surveying. Paul speaks this word to the church, which I believe that we need to flow in today, he says in 1 Thessalonians 5:12,

And we beseech you, brethren, to know them, which labour among you, and are over you in the Lord, and admonish you;

Paul, even though he admonishes the church to respect and honor its leaders, stresses that we are to know them. The Greek word here is "eido," which means to see, to be aware, to consider.

An effective intercessor will be aware of their strengths as well as their weaknesses so that they will know how to pray on their behalf. Therefore, connection is important for the success of our leaders. We will see that as we continue this discourse that Paul uses a word of relationship and connection, the word he uses is brethren. "Brethren" here is the Greek word "adelphos," which is a connective particle which leads us to the word womb, those who are birthed out of the same spirit. So it speaks to those who are connected out of a kindred Spirit.

God had given me this revelation before but it became even more clear when the Elder came forth with the revelation that every year about the same time certain issues come against the man of God and even the church of God. Certain kinds of issues surface at certain times of the year.

I believe that those who are positioned to cover our leaders can turn the attack of the enemy simply by being in the gap interceding at the right times.

I believe that the enemy releases certain spirits at certain times to disrupt the flow and anointing upon our leaders. This will cause them not to operate at full power and can ultimately decrease their ability to lead.

Paul's prayer in 2 Thessalonians 3:1 bears some looking into he says,

Finally, brethren, pray for us, that the word of the Lord may have free course, and be glorified, even as it is with you:

Sometimes the enemy uses the personal issues of leaders to block and hinder the flow of what God desires to release upon His people. There have been times in my ministry that I knew that the things that were going on in my mind and in my body was nothing but the enemy coming against the Word that was in me so that someone's personal breakthrough would be hindered, but thank God for intercessors who cover the man of God so that in spite of the plots of the enemy the work of the Lord prevails.

So, Paul shows us here three things; the need to pray for leaders, our ability to stop and to hinder the attack of the enemy and how God can use those who stand in the Gap to enhance the ministry of a leader.

As we look at the need to pray for our leaders many don't understand how vital this is. This is so important because so many people think or are under the impression that leaders have it all together. Paul exposes his weakness and the weakness of all leaders when he says pray for me. His cry was 'I need prayer too'.

The cry in 1 Thessalonians 5:25 was simply *Brethren, pray for us*, likewise in Hebrews 13:18 he says *Pray for us: for we trust we have An Effective conscience, in all things willing to live honestly.*

The cry of the apostle leads us to understand that Christian leaders are not "super saints" that have it all going on and that even the best of leaders have the ability to miss what God is doing and saying in a particular time and season; this was expressed even in the life of Christ as he walked these mundane shores.

Hebrews 4:15 Paul concludes,

For we have not an high priest which cannot be touched with the feeling of our infirmities; but was in all points tempted like as we are, yet without sin. Leaders just like all others go through he stresses and the pains of life.

Paul opens to us the reality that we have through prayer and intercession the ability to stop and to hinder the attack of the enemy.

We have the power and the ability to alter the course and plan put out by the enemy. Paul says pray for us. We believe that there is power in prayer, that God hears the prayers and even the groans of the saints. We prevail when we intercede. 2 Thessalonians 3:1-3 says,

Finally, brethren, pray for us, that the word of the Lord may have free course, and be glorified, even as it is with you: And that we may be delivered from unreasonable and wicked men: for all men have not faith. But the Lord is faithful, who shall stablish you, and keep you from evil.

1 Thessalonians 2:18 says,

Wherefore we would have come unto you, even I Paul, once and again; but Satan hindered us.

You could say that without this intercession there would be little to no ministry of leaders without those to uplift them in prayer. God can really use those who stand in the gap to enhance the ministry of a leader.

I believe that my ministry would not be what it is today had not intercessors been praying for me. I believe that without a shadow of a doubt that I am better when people pray. God petitions the intercessor to pray that the Word would have free course, that the enemy would not be able to hold the word up or clog it up inside of God's vessel.

I believe that God positions intercessors with leaders. He places certain leaders in the hearts of certain intercessors. He reveals those things to them that not everyone else will know. I believe that God calls and connects certain intercessors to pray and to cover certain leaders. This is vitally important because many are out of place because they didn't know how to respond to what God showed them about a leader. The call to cover is one that must be approached with much maturity. As An effective intercessor we must ask ourselves are we ready to walk in this powerful, yet sacred place of intercession. I believe that is one of God highest calls, the call to intercession, the call to pray for and cover our spiritual leaders.

This call is not to place the intercessor above leadership, but to surround leadership with Godly influence and wisdom from above that alerts and protects from the attack of the enemy. There is a powerful lesson here mainly that God is not working behind us, He's working before us. God is always walking in the Spirit before the leader; therefore, He positions intercessors to pray and to cover before the enemy attacks. God already knows that the attack is coming, so He doesn't allow the enemy to attack first, He first exposes the plot of the enemy to those who are in place, in the gap, so that they might intercede on behalf of a leader.

It is through prayer and intercession that we are able to turn what the enemy has meant for evil into good. I wonder what would have happen to Peter had not Jesus been interceding on his behalf. I think that even though Peter could have handled the situation better but that was not the prayer, the prayer was *I pray that your faith fail not.* Peter's faith did not fail; therefore, he was able to go forth and be a blessing to others. Thank God for the Jesus the great intercessor. Because of Peter's faith staying strong the establishment of the church and the Word of God weren't prevented.

Conclusion

Leaders, their decisions and examples will often determine the outcome of a battle. If we can pray our leaders through, then we know that our personal defeat of the enemy is attainable and at hand. As we push and pray our leaders through, we also go through with our leaders. As he opens the door for victory and breakthrough it is not only for the leader, but it is a signal that we have this victory and breakthrough as well; this signals to the whole nation, the whole church that victory is in the house. It is incumbent upon the intercessors to break the leader through so that all may prosper. When demons and all kinds of Spirits fall, it sends a signal that the way is clear. When one falls he doesn't fall alone, as we breakthrough in one area other areas fall. This is all released through the intercessor praying for their leaders.

THE FIVE TRAITS PRAYER

Father, I ask you right now to make me an effective intercessor. Help me to always pray because I have disciplined myself to do so. Help me to commit to my set times and places for prayer. Help me to be diligent in prayer because I understand that this is my duty as a Believer. Father, help me to not only be disciplined in prayer but in my flesh as well. Help me to maintain proper eating and sleeping habits so that I may be eager and alert for prayer. Father, make my temple your home and dwell there freely without hindrance.

Father, help me to flow in the Spirit. Lead me and give me discernment through your precious Holy Spirit. Let me know the mind of Christ as I pray and let me feel your heart concerning my prayers. Father, let me move always in your Spirit and not in the Spirit of error. Let me always judge the motive and intents of my prayers through your Spirit. Give me the wisdom to discern the difference. Let my motives for prayer always proceed from the active fruit of the Spirit in my life. Help me to produce even more as I go deeper in you.

Father, make me ever watchful as I position myself to hear from you. Let me not have a Spirit of slumber or blindness but that of the watchman who is ever at his post. Help me to be sensitive to your Spirit and your voice as you shift and move on behalf of your people.

Father, I surrender my flesh to you. Help me to always empty myself so that I may pray effectively, not my will Lord, but yours. I will not pray selfishly but will turn my compassion out towards others that they may be covered in prayer.

Father, help me to keep my Man or Woman of God covered in prayer. Help me to see the signs of the enemy as he attempts to take them out. Show me how to pray and help me to not become trapped by thinking more highly of myself than I ought because of this insight.

I thank you that all that I have gleaned will stick in my heart and that I will be an effective intercessor.

In Jesus' Name, Amen

Made in the USA
Columbia, SC
17 December 2025

76236034R00046